ALL NEW
SIMPLE & ELEGANT
RECIPES

A WORD ABOUT "PHILLY"

PHILADELPHIA BRAND Cream Cheese products ..... for the way we live today.

American Moms and other great chefs have been baking, cooking and entertaining with PHILADELPHIA BRAND Cream Cheese for generations and "PHILLY" Cream Cheese is still America's favorite! It's the perfect ingredient for a variety of foods from appetizers and side dishes to main meal fare and desserts. "PHILLY" Cream Cheese products add a real touch of elegance to even the simplest of recipes.

The versatility of "PHILLY" Cream Cheese products makes them a natural for today's cooking. The smooth creamy texture can be spread, blended, melted, baked, cooked or simply topped on your favorite dish. And today you'll find "PHILLY" Cream Cheese products in a variety of convenient forms to fit all your needs. You know that the PHILADEPHIA BRAND Cream Cheese brick has always been ideal for baking and cooking. But did you know that you can substitute Light PHILADEPHIA BRAND Neufchatel Cheese brick in your recipes and still get that creamy delicious taste with 25% less fat?

Although it was developed to be and is most often used as a spreading cheese, PHILADELPHIA BRAND Soft Cream Cheese is suitable for many recipes. You'll especially like the easy blending qualities of "PHILLY" Cream Cheese when preparing quick chilled recipes such as dips, spreads, frostings, cold sauces or fillings. In recipes calling for brick cream cheese, soft cream cheese should not be substituted because a softer consistency may result.

Whatever the occasion, "PHILLY" Cream Cheese products help make the most of it!

Everybody's Got a Soft Spot for "PHILLY" Soft Cream Cheese Flavors!

One taste and you'll know why "PHILLY" Soft Cream Cheese Flavors combine smooth, creamy PHILADELPHIA BRAND Cream Cheese with natural flavors to create a potpourri of delicious tastes. They're easy to spread and add a unique flavor to recipes, too.

Best of all, "PHILLY" Soft Cream Cheese Flavors are deliciously versatile. Imagine delicious "PHILLY" Soft Cream Cheese with Strawberries spread over pound cake and sugar cookies. Or savory "PHILLY" Soft Cream Cheese with Chive & Onion topped on a piping hot baked potato. Spreading "PHILLY" Soft Cream Cheese with Pineapple over an ordinary waffle makes it . . . . extraordinary. And "PHILLY" Soft Cream Cheese with Herb & Garlic tossed with steaming hot pasta gives an old favorite a new twist. A variety of flavors means you'll never run out of delicious ideas.

To give you a start, we've included a sampling of elegant recipes using "PHILLY" Soft Cream Cheese Flavors in this book—everything from appetizers to desserts. But with a little of your own imagination, the possibilities are endless!

Whatever the occasion, "PHILLY" Cream Cheese products help you make the most of it!

APPETIZERS & SNACKS

What makes these starters so special is PHILADELPHIA BRAND Cream Cheese. Whether you are seeking an imaginative appetizer for entertaining or a satisfying everyday snack, just flip the page for a variety of intriguing recipes.

BACON APPETIZER CRESCENTS

For extra convenience, prepare the filling in advance.

   1 8-oz. pkg. PHILADELPHIA BRAND Cream
        Cheese, softened
   8 OSCAR MAYER Bacon Slices, crisply
        cooked, crumbled
   ⅓ cup (1½ ozs.) KRAFT 100% Grated
        Parmesan Cheese
   ¼ cup finely chopped onion
   2 tablespoons chopped parsley
   1 tablespoon milk
   2 8-oz. cans PILLSBURY Refrigerated Quick
        Crescent Dinner Rolls
   1 egg, beaten
   1 teaspoon cold water

- Preheat oven to 375°.
- Beat cream cheese, bacon, parmesan cheese,
  onion, parsley and milk in small mixing bowl at
  medium speed with electric mixer until well
  blended.
- Separate dough into eight rectangles; firmly
  press perforations together to seal. Spread each
  rectangle with 2 rounded measuring
  tablespoonfuls cream cheese mixture.
- Cut each rectangle in half diagonally; repeat
  with opposite corners. Cut in half crosswise to
  form six triangles. Roll up triangles, starting at
  short ends.
- Place on greased cookie sheet; brush with
  combined egg and water. Sprinkle with poppy
  seed, if desired.
- Bake 12 to 15 minutes or until golden brown.
  Serve immediately.

                    Approximately 4 dozen appetizers

Prep time: 30 minutes
Cooking time: 15 minutes

THREE PEPPER QUESADILLAS

For extra convenience, assemble these quesadillas in advance.

1 cup thin green pepper strips
1 cup thin red pepper strips
1 cup thin yellow pepper strips
½ cup thin onion slices
⅓ cup PARKAY Margarine
½ teaspoon ground cumin
1 8-oz. pkg. PHILADELPHIA BRAND Cream Cheese, softened
1 8-oz. pkg. 100% Natural KRAFT Shredded Sharp Cheddar Cheese
½ cup (2 ozs.) KRAFT 100% Grated Parmesan Cheese
10 6-inch flour tortillas

- Preheat oven to 425°.
- Saute peppers and onions in margarine in large skillet. Stir in cumin. Drain, reserving liquid.
- Beat cheeses in small mixing bowl at medium speed with electric mixer until well blended.
- Spoon 2 tablespoons cheese mixture onto each tortilla; top with pepper mixture. Fold tortillas in half; place on baking sheet. Brush with reserved liquid.
- Bake 10 minutes. Cut each tortilla into thirds. Serve warm with salsa.   *30 appetizers*

Prep time: 20 minutes
Cooking time: 10 minutes

Tip: To make ahead, prepare as directed except for baking. Cover; refrigerate. When ready to serve, bake at 425°, 15 to 20 minutes or until thoroughly heated.

European cucumbers are longer than ordinary cucumbers. They are seedless and require no peeling.

HERBED CUCUMBER CANAPES

Quick, easy and attractive ... the essential elements of weekday entertaining. The "PHILLY" Cream Cheese spread can be prepared in advance and chilled until ready to serve.

    1 8-oz. pkg. PHILADELPHIA BRAND Cream
        Cheese, softened
    2 garlic cloves, minced
    ½ cup green onion slices
    ½ cup chopped parsley
    ½ teaspoon dried thyme leaves, crushed
    ½ teaspoon salt
    ¼ teaspoon pepper
    ¼ teaspoon dried tarragon leaves, crushed
    1 English or European cucumber, cut into
        ⅛ to ¼-inch slices

- Beat all ingredients except cucumber in large mixing bowl at medium speed with electric mixer until well blended.
- Spread cucumber slices with cream cheese mixture. Garnish with assorted vegetables and fresh herbs, if desired.

Approximately 3½ dozen

Prep time: 20 minutes

Variation: Substitute PHILADELPHIA BRAND Light Neufchatel Cheese for cream cheese.

HOT AND SPICY CHICKEN NUGGETS

This creamy salsa dip is a natural accompaniment for popular chicken nuggets.

    1 8-oz. container PHILADELPHIA BRAND
        Soft Cream Cheese
    ½ cup salsa
    2 tablespoons milk
    ½ teaspoon ground cumin
    ½ teaspoon onion powder
    ½ teaspoon garlic powder
    ¼ to ½ teaspoon cayenne pepper
    2 10.5-oz. pkgs. frozen chicken nuggets

- Stir together all ingredients except chicken nuggets in small bowl until well blended. Chill.
- Prepare chicken nuggets according to package directions. Serve with cream cheese dip.

Approximately 3 dozen

Prep time: 10 minutes plus chilling
Cooking time: Approximately 20 minutes

HOT CHEESY ALMOND SPREAD

You may want to double the recipe for any appetizer party... this favorite disappears rapidly!

    1 8-oz. pkg. PHILADELPHIA BRAND Cream
        Cheese, softened
1½ cups (6 ozs.) shredded 100% Natural
        KRAFT Swiss Cheese
    ⅓ cup KRAFT Real Mayonnaise
    ¼ cup chopped green onion
    ⅛ teaspoon ground nutmeg
    ⅛ teaspoon pepper
    ¼ cup sliced almonds, toasted

- Preheat oven to 350°.
- Beat all ingredients except almonds in small mixing bowl at medium speed with electric mixer until well blended. Stir in almonds. Spread into 9-inch pie plate.
- Bake 15 minutes, stirring after 8 minutes. Garnish with additional toasted sliced almonds, if desired. Serve with assorted crackers or party rye bread slices.   *2⅓ cups*

Prep time: 15 minutes
Cooking time: 15 minutes

MICROWAVE: • Prepare recipe as directed except for baking. • Microwave on MEDIUM (50%) 6 minutes or until Swiss cheese is melted and mixture is warm, stirring after 4 minutes. (Do not overcook.) • Stir before serving. Garnish with additional toasted sliced almonds, if desired. Serve with assorted crackers or party rye bread slices.

SOUTHWESTERN CHEESECAKE

To make an attractive design on top of this cheesecake, simply cut three diamonds out of paper. Place on top of cheesecake. Place green onion slices around diamonds. Remove cutouts; fill in with peppers. Add a strip of tomatoes down the center. Garnish with olives.

All of your favorite southwestern ingredients in a savory cheesecake ... fantastic looking and tasting!

> 1 cup finely crushed tortilla chips
> 3 tablespoons PARKAY Margarine, melted
> 2 8-oz. pkgs. PHILADELPHIA BRAND
>   Cream Cheese, softened
> 2 eggs
> 1 8-oz. pkg. 100% Natural KRAFT Shredded
>   Colby/Monterey Jack Cheese
> 1 4-oz. can chopped green chilies, drained
> 1 cup sour cream
> 1 cup chopped yellow or orange pepper
> ½ cup green onion slices
> ⅓ cup chopped tomatoes
> ¼ cup pitted ripe olive slices

- Preheat oven to 325°.
- Stir together chips and margarine in small bowl; press onto bottom of 9-inch springform pan. Bake 15 minutes.
- Beat cream cheese and eggs in large mixing bowl at medium speed with electric mixer until well blended. Mix in shredded cheese and chilies; pour over crust. Bake 30 minutes.
- Spread sour cream over cheesecake. Loosen cake from rim of pan; cool before removing rim of pan. Chill.
- Top with remaining ingredients just before serving.

16 to 20 servings

Prep time: 20 minutes plus chilling
Cooking time: 30 minutes

ZESTY CORNCAKES

A savory variation of corn fritters, these versatile corncakes are delicious served as appetizers, snacks or main dish accompaniments.

For easy handling, roll formed balls in cornmeal; flatten in skillet with back of spatula.

2 8-oz. pkgs PHILADELPHIA BRAND Cream Cheese, softened
¼ cup green onion slices
Salsa
1 egg
1 10-oz. pkg. BIRDS EYE Sweet Corn, thawed, drained
⅔ cup (3 ozs.) 100% Natural KRAFT Shredded Sharp Cheddar Cheese
Cornmeal
¼ cup flour
1 teaspoon CALUMET Baking Powder
1 teaspoon salt
2 tablespoons PARKAY Margarine
2 tablespoons oil

- Beat cream cheese and onions in large mixing bowl at medium speed with electric mixer until well blended.
- Divide mixture in half; reserve one half for topping. Add ⅓ cup salsa and egg to remaining half, mixing until well blended.
- Stir in corn, cheddar cheese, ⅓ cup cornmeal, flour, baking powder and salt.
- Roll heaping tablespoonfuls of corn mixture in additional cornmeal.
- Flatten dough into patties. Brown in combined margarine and oil in large skillet; turn once.
- Serve warm with reserved cream cheese mixture and additional salsa.

Approximately 2 dozen appetizers

Prep time: 30 minutes
Cooking time: 15 minutes

Shell and devein shrimp before cooking. To cook one pound of shrimp, combine 1 cup cold water, 1 cup dry white wine, 2 to 3 peppercorns, 1 bay leaf and 3 to 4 lemon slices; bring to a boil. Add shrimp; reduce heat and simmer 3 to 5 minutes. Drain. Chill.

SHRIMP AND CHINESE PEA PODS

The unique dip is a zesty blend of "PHILLY" Cream Cheese, watercress, mayonnaise and lemon juice.

1½ cups packed watercress leaves
 1 8-oz. pkg. PHILADELPHIA BRAND Cream Cheese, softened
 ¼ cup green onion slices
1½ tablespoons lemon juice
 ¼ teaspoon salt
 ¼ cup KRAFT Real Mayonnaise
1½ lbs. cleaned medium shrimp, cooked
 ½ lb. Chinese pea pods, blanched
 1 red pepper, cut into thin strips
 1 leek, cut into thin strips

- Place all ingredients except shrimp, pea pods, peppers and leek in food processor or blender container; process until well blended. Chill.
- Wrap shrimp with pea pod; garnish with peppers. Tie knot with leek to secure. Serve with watercress sauce.

Approximately 3 dozen appetizers

Prep time: 45 minutes plus chilling

Tip: Omit leeks and pepper strips. Secure with wooden picks.

HERB & GARLIC BITES

Finely chopped ham or crisply-cooked bacon, crumbled, are delicious alternatives for pepperoni.

 2 7.5-oz. cans PILLSBURY Refrigerated Buttermilk Biscuits
 1 8-oz. container PHILADELPHIA BRAND Soft Cream Cheese with Herb & Garlic
 6 ozs. pepperoni, finely chopped
 1 egg, beaten

Shrimp and Chinese Pea Pods

- Preheat oven to 400°.
- Separate each biscuit in half. Gently stretch dough to form 3-inch circles.
- Stir together cream cheese and pepperoni in small bowl until well blended. Spoon 1½ teaspoons cream cheese mixture onto center of each circle. Fold in half; press edges together to seal.
- Place on cookie sheet. Brush with egg. Bake 8 to 10 minutes or until golden brown. Serve immediately.   *40 appetizers*

Prep time: 10 minutes
Cooking time: 10 minutes

TORTA CALIFORNIA

This festive molded appetizer features a savory blend of "PHILLY" Cream Cheese, goat cheese and thyme, layered with bright green pesto and roasted red peppers... very Italian.

> 2 8-oz. pkgs. PHILADELPHIA BRAND
>   Cream Cheese, softened
> 1 8-oz. pkg. goat cheese
> 1 to 2 garlic cloves
> 2 tablespoons olive oil
> 1 teaspoon dried thyme leaves, crushed
> 3 tablespoons pesto, well drained
> ⅓ cup roasted red peppers, drained, chopped

- Line 1-quart souffle dish or loaf pan with plastic wrap.
- Place cream cheese, goat cheese and garlic in food processor or blender container; process until well blended. Add oil and thyme; blend well.
- Place one-third of cheese mixture in souffle dish; cover with pesto, half of remaining cheese mixture and peppers. Top with remaining cheese mixture. Cover; chill.
- Unmold; remove plastic wrap. Smooth sides. Garnish with fresh herbs and additional red pepper, if desired. Serve with assorted crackers or French bread.   *3 cups*

Prep time: 15 minutes plus chilling

Torta California

BREADSTICKS BELLISIMA

A great snack... simple and unique!

Thin boiled ham slices
PHILADELPHIA BRAND Soft Cream
   Cheese with Herb & Garlic
Breadsticks
Fresh basil leaves

- Spread each ham slice with cream cheese; cut lengthwise into ½-inch strips. Wrap ham around breadsticks. Garnish with basil leaves.

SPICY COEUR A LA CREME

A variation on a classic French delicacy, this appetizer version will add pizzazz to any party.

3 8-oz. pkgs. PHILADELPHIA BRAND
   Cream Cheese, softened
½ cup chopped green onion
2 garlic cloves, minced
1 teaspoon ground cumin
½ teaspoon salt
2 tablespoons chopped cilantro (optional)
   Dash of cayenne pepper (optional)
⅓ cup salsa

- Place all ingredients except salsa in food processor or blender container; process until well blended.
- Line coeur a la creme or 3-cup mold with cheesecloth or plastic wrap. Pour in cream cheese mixture. Cover with cheesecloth or plastic wrap. Chill several hours or overnight.
- Unwrap top of mold. Unmold; carefully remove cheesecloth or plastic wrap.
- Top with salsa. Garnish with sprig of cilantro, if desired. Serve with tortilla chips.

Approximately 2½ cups

Prep time: 20 minutes plus chilling

CREAMY ITALIAN GARLIC SPREAD

1 12-oz. container PHILADELPHIA BRAND
    Soft Cream Cheese
¼ cup PARKAY Margarine
3 garlic cloves, minced
2 tablespoons dry white wine
1½ tablespoons chopped parsley
1 tablespoon finely chopped fresh thyme or
    ½ teaspoon dried thyme leaves, crushed
1 tablespoon finely chopped fresh basil or
    ½ teaspoon dried basil leaves, crushed
    Dash of salt and pepper

- Beat cream cheese, margarine and garlic in small mixing bowl at medium speed with electric mixer until well blended.
- Blend in remaining ingredients. Chill several hours or overnight. Serve with French bread slices, toasted pita wedges or bagel chips.

2 cups

Prep time: 15 minutes plus chilling

Fresh herbs create a new flavor sensation in foods. They add personality and dimension to a dish. PHILADELPHIA BRAND Cream Cheese is a delicious way to familiarize yourself with the flavor of fresh herbs. When using fresh herbs in place of dried, use 1 tablespoon fresh for every ½ teaspoon crushed herbs. Let the herb-cheese mixture stand at least 1 hour for flavors to blend.

STUFFED POTATO APPETIZERS

1½ lbs. (24) small new red potatoes
1 8-oz. container PHILADELPHIA BRAND
    Soft Cream Cheese with Herb & Garlic
¼ cup chopped parsley

- Cook potatoes in boiling water in large saucepan 18 to 20 minutes or until tender. Drain; cool.
- Scoop out centers with melon baller or small pointed teaspoon, leaving ⅛-inch shell.
- Spoon or pipe cream cheese into potatoes. Sprinkle with parsley.   *2 dozen appetizers*

Prep time: 45 minutes

SALSA CORN CHOWDER

For a hearty entree, add chopped cooked chicken or ham to this savory chowder. Serve with cornbread or tortillas.

1½ cups chopped onion
2 tablespoons PARKAY Margarine
1 tablespoon flour
1 tablespoon chili powder
1 teaspoon ground cumin
1 16-oz. pkg. BIRDS EYE Sweet Corn, thawed
2 cups salsa
1 13¾-oz. can chicken broth
1 4-oz. jar chopped pimento, drained
1 8-oz. container PHILADELPHIA BRAND Soft Cream Cheese
1 cup milk
Cilantro

- Saute onions in margarine in large saucepan. Stir in flour and seasonings.
- Add corn, salsa, broth and pimento. Bring to boil; remove from heat.
- Gradually add ¼ cup hot mixture to cream cheese in small bowl, stirring until well blended.
- Add cream cheese mixture and milk to saucepan, stirring until well blended.
- Cook until thoroughly heated. Do not boil. Top each serving with sprig of cilantro. Serve immediately.

6 to 8 servings

Prep time: 35 minutes

MICROWAVE: • Microwave onions and margarine in 3-quart casserole on HIGH 2 to 3 minutes or until onions are tender. • Stir in flour and seasonings. • Add salsa and broth; mix well. • Microwave on HIGH 8 to 10 minutes or until mixture begins to boil, stirring after 5 minutes. • Stir in corn and pimento. • Add ¼ cup hot mixture to cream cheese in small bowl, stirring until well blended. • Add cream cheese mixture and milk to corn mixture. • Microwave on HIGH 12 to 17 minutes, or until thoroughly heated, stirring after 9 minutes. Do not boil. • Top each serving with cilantro. Serve immediately.

HERB ARTICHOKE SPREAD

1 8-oz. container PHILADELPHIA BRAND
    Soft Cream Cheese with Herb & Garlic
1 6½-oz. jar marinated artichoke hearts,
    drained, chopped
¼ teaspoon salt
4 to 6 drops hot pepper sauce

• Stir together ingredients in small bowl until well
blended. Chill. Serve with toasted bread cutouts.
Garnish with fresh herbs and chopped red
pepper, if desired.   *1½ cups*

Prep time: 5 minutes plus chilling

Tip: Cut bread slices with 2-inch cookie cutters.
Bake at 325°, 5 minutes per side or until lightly
toasted.

TURKISH CHEESE

*Flaky layers of phyllo dough are baked with a
creamy filling of four cheeses and seasonings for
this tasty appetizer treat.*

1 8-oz. pkg. PHILADELPHIA BRAND Cream
    Cheese, softened
2 eggs
¼ cup green onion slices
1 tablespoon fresh dill weed or ½ teaspoon
    dried dill weed
1 tablespoon packed chopped fresh mint
    leaves or ½ teaspoon dried mint leaves,
    crushed
1 8-oz. pkg. feta cheese, crumbled
1 cup (4 ozs.) shredded CASINO Natural
    Monterey Jack Cheese
¼ cup (1 oz.) KRAFT 100% Grated Parmesan
    Cheese
16 sheets frozen phyllo dough, thawed
¾ cup PARKAY Margarine, melted

*Phyllo is a paper-thin
Middle Eastern
strudel dough. Fresh
or frozen dough is
available in many
supermarkets. It is
important to cover
unused phyllo dough
with damp paper
towels during
assembly as the dough
dries out very quickly.*

Herb Artichoke Spread

- Preheat oven to 375°.
- Beat cream cheese, eggs, onions, dill weed and mint in small mixing bowl at medium speed with electric mixer until well blended. Stir in remaining cheeses.
- Place one phyllo sheet on 15×10×1-inch jelly roll pan; brush with margarine. Continue layering seven sheets, brushing each sheet with margarine. (Note: Dough will extend over edge of pan.)
- Spread cheese mixture over phyllo; fold edges over cheese mixture. Layer remaining phyllo sheets over cheese mixture, brushing each sheet with margarine. Tuck edges under bottom layer; drizzle with remaining margarine.
- Bake 35 to 40 minutes or until lightly browned. Cut into diamond shapes.

2 dozen appetizers

Prep time: 50 minutes
Cooking time: 40 minutes

Radicchio is a salad ingredient that is shaped like a small head of cabbage. It is red with white veins. It goes well with a variety of salad greens and is a nice compliment to a flavorful dressing.

CAVIAR-FILLED VEGETABLES

There are many flavorful options for caviar... try minced clams, baby shrimp, chopped nuts, shredded carrots or chopped red pepper.

1 8-oz. container PHILADELPHIA BRAND
    Soft Cream Cheese
1 to 2 shallots, chopped
1 tablespoon olive oil
¼ teaspoon coarsely ground black pepper
    Assorted vegetables
    Caviar

- Place cream cheese, shallots, oil and pepper in food processor or blender container; process until well blended.
- Spoon or pipe cream cheese mixture over vegetables; top with caviar. Garnish with fresh herbs, if desired.

Approximately 2 dozen appetizers

Prep Time: 10 minutes

Caviar-Filled Vegetables

SALMON CUCUMBER MOUSSE

Deliciously light and creamy, this molded mousse is an elegant buffet attraction for Spring entertaining.

    2 envelopes unflavored gelatin
    1 cup cold water
    2 tablespoons lemon juice
    2 8-oz. containers PHILADELPHIA BRAND
        Soft Cream Cheese with Smoked Salmon
    1 small cucumber, peeled, finely chopped

- Soften gelatin in water in small saucepan; stir over low heat until dissolved. Stir in lemon juice.
- Stir together cream cheese, gelatin mixture and cucumber in small bowl until well blended. Pour into lightly oiled 1-quart mold.
- Chill until firm. Unmold onto serving platter. Serve with melba toast rounds.

3 cups

Prep time: 15 minutes plus chilling

COCONUT CHEESE SPREAD

A delicious spread to keep on hand, ready in an instant for guests or a quick snack.

    1 8-oz. container PHILADELPHIA BRAND
        Soft Cream Cheese with Pineapple
    ½ cup BAKER'S ANGEL FLAKE Coconut
    ¼ cup macadamia nuts, coarsely chopped
    ½ teaspoon ground ginger

- Stir together ingredients in small bowl until well blended. Serve with apple slices and date nut or brown bread slices.   *1 cup*

Prep Time: 10 minutes

Salmon Cucumber Mousse

Quickly rinse feta cheese with water to remove salt. Drain thoroughly before crumbling.

GARDEN GREEK APPETIZER

The "PHILLY" Cream Cheese base for this attractive appetizer can be prepared several days in advance, covered tightly and chilled. Near serving time, add the colorful fresh vegetables and arrange the crackers around the edge.

> 1 8-oz. pkg. Light PHILADELPHIA BRAND Neufchatel Cheese, softened
> 1 8-oz. pkg. feta cheese, crumbled
> 2 tablespoons plain yogurt
> 1 tablespoon packed chopped fresh mint leaves or ½ teaspoon dried mint leaves, crushed
> 1 garlic clove, minced
> 1 tomato, seeded, diced
> 1 small cucumber, diced
> 1 green onion, sliced

- Beat neufchatel cheese, feta cheese, yogurt, mint and garlic in small mixing bowl at medium speed with electric mixer until well blended.
- Spread cheese mixture into 10-inch tart pan or pie plate. Chill. Top with tomatoes, cucumbers and onions just before serving. Serve with crackers or toasted pita bread wedges.

10 to 12 servings

Prep time: 15 minutes plus chilling

CLASSIC DIP

> 1 8-oz. container PHILADELPHIA BRAND Soft Cream Cheese
> 1 0.6-oz. pkg. GOOD SEASONS Zesty Italian Salad Dressing Mix
> 1 8-oz. container plain yogurt
> 1 tablespoon milk

- Stir together ingredients in small bowl until well blended. Chill. Serve with assorted vegetable dippers.

1 cup

Prep time: 10 minutes plus chilling

Garden Greek Appetizer

ENTREES & SALADS

Saucy pastas, layered casseroles, refreshing salads ... the creamy, rich flavor of PHILADELPHIA BRAND Cream Cheese adds an exciting twist to many dishes. For everyday dining or special entertaining, try these "PHILLY" Cream Cheese recipes.

Mango is a tropical fruit with a delicate floral fragrance and sweet flavor. It should ripen at room temperature; it is soft to the touch when ready to eat. To peel, score the mango lengthwise and remove a portion of the peel. There is a large flat pit inside; pry the fruit slice away from the pit. Repeat with remaining fruit.

CARIBBEAN FRUIT SALAD

1 8-oz. container PHILADELPHIA BRAND
   Soft Cream Cheese with Pineapple
½ cup pineapple juice
1 pt. strawberries, sliced
4 kiwi, peeled, sliced
2 oranges, peeled, sectioned
1 mango, peeled, cubed
1 starfruit, sliced
   Peeled cantaloupe slices
   Peeled honeydew melon slices
½ cup BAKER'S ANGEL FLAKE Coconut,
   toasted

- Stir together cream cheese and pineapple juice in small bowl until well blended; chill.
- Arrange fruit on individual salad plates. Top with cream cheese dressing. Sprinkle with coconut.

8 servings

Prep time: 20 minutes plus chilling

HAM AND CHEESE CASSEROLE

1 10-oz. pkg. BIRDS EYE Pasta Primavera
   Style Recipe Vegetables in a Seasoned
   Sauce
1 8-oz. pkg. PHILADELPHIA BRAND Cream
   Cheese, cubed
⅓ cup milk
1½ cups (¾ lb.) cubed ham
⅓ cup cheese flavored crackers, crushed

- Preheat oven to 350°.
- Cook vegetable mixture, cream cheese and milk in medium saucepan on medium-high heat until cream cheese is melted, stirring occasionally. Stir in ham.
- Spoon into 1½-quart casserole; top with crackers. Bake 25 minutes.

4 servings

Prep time: 20 minutes
Cooking time: 25 minutes

Caribbean Fruit Salad

SALMON TORTELLINI

This creamy tortellini can be served as a main dish with a variety of colorful fresh vegetables or as an accompaniment for poultry or seafood.

> 1 7-oz. pkg. cheese tortellini, cooked, drained
> 1 8-oz. container PHILADELPHIA BRAND
>   Soft Cream Cheese with Smoked Salmon
> ½ cup finely chopped cucumber
> 1 teaspoon dried dill weed or 2 teaspoons
>   fresh dill weed

- Lightly toss hot tortellini with remaining ingredients. Serve immediately.

6 to 8 servings

Prep time: 30 minutes

TURKEY PASTA SALAD

> 1 8-oz. pkg. shell macaroni, cooked, drained
> 2 cups cubed cooked turkey
> 1 cup celery slices
> ½ cup chopped red pepper
> 2 tablespoons chopped parsley
> 1 8-oz. container PHILADELPHIA BRAND
>   Soft Cream Cheese with Chives & Onion
> ¾ cup sour cream
> ¼ cup milk
> ½ teaspoon dried basil leaves, crushed
>   Salt and pepper
>   Fresh spinach leaves

- Stir together macaroni, turkey, celery, red pepper and parsley in large bowl.
- Stir together cream cheese, sour cream, milk and basil in small bowl until well blended.
- Add to macaroni mixture; toss lightly. Season with salt and pepper to taste. Chill.
- Add additional milk just before serving, if desired. Serve on spinach-lined salad plates.

8 servings

Prep time: 30 minutes plus chilling

Salmon Tortellini

Dipping tortillas in enchilada sauce prevents drying during baking.

ENCHILADAS SUIZAS

(pictured on back cover)

This spicy meatless main dish with southwestern flair is sure to become a family favorite.

> 1 8-oz. pkg. PHILADELPHIA BRAND Cream Cheese, softened
> ½ cup green onion slices
> 1½ cups (6 ozs.) shredded 100% Natural KRAFT Sharp Cheddar Cheese
> 1½ cups (6 ozs.) shredded 100% Natural KRAFT Monterey Jack Cheese
> 2 4-oz. cans chopped green chilies, drained
> ½ teaspoon ground cumin
> 3 eggs
> 12 corn tortillas
> Oil
> 2 8-oz. jars enchilada sauce
> 1 4¼-oz. can chopped pitted ripe olives

- Preheat oven to 350°.
- Beat half of cream cheese and onions in small mixing bowl at medium speed with electric mixer until well blended. Reserve for topping.
- Beat remaining cream cheese, 1¼ cups cheddar cheese, 1¼ cups Monterey Jack cheese, chilies and cumin in large mixing bowl at medium speed with electric mixer until well blended.
- Add eggs, one at a time, mixing well after each addition.
- Warm tortillas in lightly oiled skillet. Spoon 2 tablespoonfuls cheddar cheese mixture onto each tortilla; roll up.
- Place in 13×9-inch baking dish; top with enchilada sauce and remaining shredded cheeses.
- Bake 20 minutes or until thoroughly heated. Top with reserved cream cheese mixture and olives.

6 servings

Prep time: 25 minutes
Cooking time: 20 minutes

EGGPLANT BULGUR CASSEROLE

A meatless main dish and pleasant change from pasta or rice ... bulgur wheat resembles brown rice and wild rice in flavor and texture.

1 cup bulgur wheat
½ cup chopped green pepper
¼ cup chopped onion
¼ cup PARKAY Margarine
4 cups cubed peeled eggplant
1 15-oz. can tomato sauce
1 14½-oz. can tomatoes, cut up
½ cup cold water
½ teaspoon dried oregano leaves, crushed
1 8-oz. pkg. PHILADELPHIA BRAND Cream Cheese, softened
1 egg
KRAFT 100% Grated Parmesan Cheese

Bulgur, a parboiled cracked wheat, is used in Middle Eastern and Greek cuisine. It is a shelf-stable grain which comes in fine, medium and coarse textures. Like rice, it should be cooked in liquid until all of the liquid is absorbed.

- Preheat oven to 350°.
- Saute bulgur wheat, peppers and onions in margarine in large skillet until vegetables are tender.
- Stir in eggplant, tomato sauce, tomatoes, water and oregano. Cover; simmer 15 to 20 minutes or until eggplant is tender, stirring occasionally.
- Beat cream cheese and egg in small mixing bowl at medium speed with electric mixer until well blended.
- Place half of vegetable mixture in 1½-quart baking dish or casserole; top with cream cheese mixture and remaining vegetable mixture. Cover.
- Bake 15 minutes. Remove cover; sprinkle with parmesan cheese. Continue baking 10 minutes or until thoroughly heated.   *8 to 10 servings*

Prep time: 30 minutes
Cooking time: 25 minutes

MICROWAVE: • Omit water. • Microwave bulgur, peppers and onions in margarine in 2-quart casserole on HIGH 4 to 5 minutes or until vegetables are tender, stirring after 3 minutes.
• Stir in eggplant, tomato sauce, tomatoes and oregano. Cover with plastic wrap; vent.

(continued on next page)

- Microwave on HIGH 10 to 15 minutes or until eggplant is tender, stirring every 6 minutes. • Beat cream cheese and egg in small mixing bowl at medium speed with electric mixer until well blended. • Place half of vegetable mixture in 2-quart casserole; top with cream cheese mixture and remaining vegetable mixture. • Microwave on HIGH 7 to 9 minutes or until thoroughly heated. Sprinkle with parmesan cheese. Let stand 5 minutes.

FETTUCCINE WITH SUN-DRIED TOMATO CREAM

⅔ cup sun-dried tomatoes
3 to 4 garlic cloves
1 8-oz. container PHILADELPHIA BRAND Soft Cream Cheese
½ teaspoon dried oregano leaves, crushed
¼ cup PARKAY Margarine
¼ cup sour cream
1 lb. fettuccine, cooked, drained
¼ cup olive oil
  Salt and pepper
2 tablespoons chopped parsley

- Cover tomatoes with boiling water; let stand 10 minutes. Drain.
- Place tomatoes and garlic in food processor or blender container; process until coarsely chopped. Add cream cheese and oregano; process until well blended.
- Melt margarine in medium saucepan; stir in cream cheese mixture and sour cream. Cook until thoroughly heated.
- Toss hot fettuccine with oil.
- Add cream cheese mixture. Season with salt and pepper to taste. Sprinkle with chopped parsley. Serve immediately.   *8 to 10 servings*

Prep time: 30 minutes

Sun-dried tomatoes can be purchased dried or packed in oil, usually olive oil. The dry-pack tomatoes, like good quality dried fruit, should be slightly moist to the touch.

Fettuccine with Sun-Dried Tomato Cream

ELEGANT SPRINGTIME SALAD

1 8-oz. pkg. PHILADELPHIA BRAND Cream
   Cheese, softened
¼ cup (2 ozs.) KRAFT Blue Cheese Crumbles
¼ cup chopped pecans
3 OSCAR MAYER Bacon Slices, crisply
   cooked, crumbled
⅓ cup chopped parsley
2 qts. torn assorted greens
   Orange or yellow pepper strips
   Chopped red pepper
   Red onion rings
   KRAFT "Zesty" Italian Dressing

- Beat cheeses in small mixing bowl at medium
  speed with electric mixer until blended. Add
  pecans and bacon; mix well. Chill until firm.
- Shape cheese mixture into 8-inch log. Roll in
  parsley. Wrap in plastic wrap; chill.
- Slice cheese log into twenty-four slices.
- Arrange greens and vegetables on individual
  salad plates. Top each with three cheese slices.
  Serve with dressing.   *8 servings*

Prep time: 25 minutes plus chilling

Variation: Omit yellow or orange pepper strips
and onion rings. Top with carrot curls.

BRANDIED CHICKEN THIGHS
WITH MUSHROOMS

*Easy and elegant...nothing could be better for
informal entertaining.*

2½ lbs. (8 to 10) chicken thighs
   Flour
¼ cup PARKAY Margarine
2 cups mushroom slices
½ cup brandy
1 8-oz. container PHILADELPHIA BRAND
   Soft Cream Cheese with Herb & Garlic
   Salt and pepper

Elegant Springtime Salad

- Lightly coat chicken with flour. Brown chicken in margarine in large skillet; remove chicken, reserving liquid in skillet.
- Saute mushrooms in reserved liquid until tender. Stir in brandy. Return chicken to skillet. Cook, covered, 30 minutes or until tender. Place chicken on ovenproof serving platter. Cover; keep warm.
- Skim fat from liquid in skillet; discard fat. Add cream cheese to reserved liquid; stir until mixture is smooth and thoroughly heated. Season with salt and pepper to taste. Pour over chicken.   *4 to 6 servings*

Prep time: 50 minutes

BUFFET SALAD WITH BLUE CHEESE DRESSING

Arranged attractively on a large glass or ceramic platter, this gorgeous main dish salad can be the focal point of a bountiful buffet.

   1 8-oz. pkg. Light PHILADELPHIA BRAND Neufchatel Cheese, softened
   1 6-oz. pkg. KRAFT Blue Cheese, crumbled
   1 8-oz. bottle KRAFT "Zesty" Italian Dressing
   2 qts. torn assorted greens
   3 Belgian endive
   2 tablespoons lemon juice
   3 tomatoes, cut into wedges
   2 green, yellow or orange peppers, cut into strips
   2 cucumbers, thinly sliced
   1 small red onion, cut into rings
   ¼ lb. Chinese pea pods, blanched
   ¾ lb. rare roast beef, thinly sliced, cut into julienne strips

Buffet Salad with Blue Cheese Dressing

- Place neufchatel cheese and blue cheese in food processor or blender container; process until smooth. Add dressing; process until blended.
- Separate endive leaves; toss with lemon juice. Place endive and greens on large platter; top with vegetables and meat. Serve with neufchatel cheese dressing.   *10 to 12 servings*

Prep time: 25 minutes

CREAMY ORZO WITH PROSCIUTTO

This savory pasta can be served as a hearty side dish or as a main course for a light supper or luncheon.

Orzo is a tiny rice-shaped pasta. It is generally used as a soup pasta; however, Italian cooks also use this pasta in flavorful side dishes.

   2 garlic cloves, minced
   2 tablespoons PARKAY Margarine
   1 8-oz. pkg. PHILADELPHIA BRAND Cream
       Cheese, cubed
   ½ cup chicken broth
       Dash of turmeric
   1 16-oz. pkg. orzo, cooked, drained
   1 10-oz. pkg. BIRDS EYE Deluxe Tender Tiny
       Peas, thawed, drained
   3 ozs. thinly sliced prosciutto, cut into
       julienne strips
       Salt and pepper

- Saute garlic in margarine in large saucepan. Add cream cheese, broth and turmeric; stir over low heat until cream cheese is melted.
- Stir in orzo, peas and prosciutto; heat thoroughly, stirring occasionally. Season with salt and pepper to taste. Serve with parmesan cheese.   *8 to 10 servings*

Prep time: 25 minutes

Tip: Recipe can be doubled for a main dish meal.

Creamy Orzo with Prosciutto

COFFEECAKES & SWEET ROLLS

Nothing is as tempting as the aroma of freshly-baked pastries—unless it's the taste of pastries, freshly made with PHILADELPHIA BRAND Cream Cheese. "PHILLY" Cream Cheese adds a moist tender texture to cakes and a creamy consistency to fillings. You'll find a wealth of inspiration on the following pages.

BREAKFAST RAISIN RING

"PHILLY" Cream Cheese adds a delicate flavor and texture to this coffeecake and filling.

    1 8-oz. pkg. PHILADELPHIA BRAND Cream
        Cheese, cubed
    1 cup cold water
    1 16-oz. pkg. hot roll mix
    1 egg
    1 teaspoon vanilla
    ½ cup packed brown sugar
    ⅓ cup PARKAY Margarine
    ¼ cup granulated sugar
    1½ teaspoons cinnamon
    1½ teaspoons vanilla
    ½ cup golden raisins
        Vanilla Drizzle

To knead dough, place on lightly floured surface. With floured hands, fold dough toward you with fingers; push firmly away with heel of hand. Give dough a quarter turn; repeat. Add additional flour to surface as needed to prevent sticking.

- Preheat oven to 350°.
- Blend 6 ounces cream cheese and water in small saucepan. Cook over low heat until mixture reaches 115° to 120°, stirring occasionally.
- Stir together hot roll mix and yeast packet in large bowl. Add cream cheese mixture, egg and 1 teaspoon vanilla, mixing until dough pulls away from sides of bowl.
- Knead dough on lightly floured surface 5 minutes or until smooth and elastic. Cover; let rise in warm place 20 minutes.
- Beat remaining cream cheese, brown sugar, margarine, granulated sugar, cinnamon and 1½ teaspoons vanilla in small mixing bowl at medium speed with electric mixer until well blended.
- Roll out dough to 20×12-inch rectangle; spread cream cheese mixture over dough to within 1½ inches from outer edges of dough. Sprinkle with raisins.
- Roll up from long end, sealing edges. Place, seam side down, on greased cookie sheet; shape into ring, pressing ends together to seal. Make 1 inch cuts through ring from outer edge at 2 inch intervals. Cover; let rise in warm place 30 minutes.
- Bake 30 to 40 minutes or until golden brown. Cool slightly. Drizzle with Vanilla Drizzle.

8 to 10 servings

(continued on next page)

VANILLA DRIZZLE

1 cup powdered sugar
1 to 2 tablespoons milk
1 teaspoon vanilla
½ teaspoon cinnamon (optional)

- Stir ingredients together in small bowl until smooth.

Prep time: 30 minutes plus rising
Cooking time: 40 minutes

CREAM CHEESE AND PECAN DANISH

1 sheet frozen puff pastry, thawed
2 3-oz. pkgs. PHILADELPHIA BRAND
   Cream Cheese, softened
¼ cup powdered sugar
1 egg
1 teaspoon vanilla
¾ cup chopped pecans
   Creamy Glaze

- Preheat oven to 375°.
- Unfold pastry; roll to 15×10-inch rectangle. Place in 15×10×1-inch jelly roll pan.
- Beat 6 ounces cream cheese, ¼ cup sugar, egg and vanilla in small mixing bowl at medium speed with electric mixer until well blended. Stir in ½ cup pecans.
- Spread cream cheese mixture over pastry to within 3 inches from outer edges.
- Make 2 inch cuts at 1-inch intervals on long sides of pastry. Crisscross strips over filling.
- Bake 25 to 30 minutes or until golden brown. Cool.
- Drizzle with Creamy Glaze. Sprinkle with remaining pecans.   *10 to 12 servings*

CREAMY GLAZE

1 3-oz. pkg. PHILADELPHIA BRAND Cream
   Cheese, softened
¾ cup powdered sugar
1 tablespoon milk

- Beat ingredients until smooth.

Prep time: 20 minutes
Cooking time: 30 minutes

BANANA-SCOTCH BREAKFAST CAKE

1 8-oz. pkg. PHILADELPHIA BRAND Cream
  Cheese, softened
⅓ cup oil
2 eggs
½ teaspoon vanilla
½ cup cold water
1 14-oz. pkg. banana bread mix
½ cup chopped pecans, toasted
½ cup currants
1½ cups butterscotch artificial flavored morsels
  Powdered sugar

- Preheat oven to 350°.
- Beat cream cheese, oil, eggs and vanilla in large mixing bowl at medium speed with electric mixer until well blended. Gradually blend in water.
- Stir in bread mix, mixing just until moistened. Fold in pecans and currants. Pour into greased and floured 13×9-inch baking pan.
- Sprinkle with butterscotch morsels; gently press into batter.
- Bake 35 minutes or until wooden pick inserted in center comes out clean. Cool. Sprinkle lightly with powdered sugar just before serving.

12 servings

Prep time: 20 minutes
Cooking time: 35 minutes

EASTER BUNS WITH VANILLA GLAZE

A special Easter treat... "PHILLY" Soft Cream Cheese with pineapple and piña colada yogurt add the unique rich flavor and texture to these delicious rolls.

1 8-oz. container PHILADELPHIA BRAND
    Soft Cream Cheese with Pineapple
1 8-oz. container pina colada flavored yogurt
2 tablespoons PARKAY Margarine
1 16-oz. pkg. hot roll mix
⅓ cup granulated sugar
1 egg
    Vanilla Glaze

- Preheat oven to 350°.
- Stir together cream cheese, yogurt and margarine in small saucepan until well blended. Cook over low heat until mixture reaches 115° to 120°, stirring occasionally.
- Stir together hot roll mix, yeast packet and granulated sugar in large bowl. Add cream cheese mixture and egg, mixing until dough pulls away from sides of bowl.
- Knead dough on lightly floured surface 5 minutes or until smooth and elastic. Cover; let rise in warm place 20 minutes.
- Divide dough into twenty-four balls. Place 2 inches apart on greased cookie sheet. Cut crisscross design with knife on top of balls, ½ inch deep. Cover; let rise in warm place 30 minutes.
- Bake 20 to 22 minutes or until lightly browned. Dip warm buns into Vanilla Glaze.

2 dozen

VANILLA GLAZE

1½ cups powdered sugar
  3 tablespoons light corn syrup
  3 tablespoons cold water
  2 teaspoons vanilla

- Stir together ingredients in small bowl until smooth.

Prep time: 30 minutes plus rising
Cooking time: 22 minutes

Tough muffins full of holes are the result of overmixing. For tender muffins, make a well in the combined dry ingredients. Pour combined liquids, all at once, into the well. Stir just enough to moisten dry ingredients. Do not overmix.

HOMESTYLE BLUEBERRY MUFFINS

"PHILLY"Cream Cheese makes these much more than "just muffins".

> 1 8-oz. pkg. PHILADELPHIA BRAND Cream Cheese, softened
> ¼ cup sugar
> 1 egg yolk
> 1 teaspoon vanilla
> 1 23.5-oz. pkg. bakery style blueberry muffin mix
> ¾ cup water
> 1 egg
> 1 teaspoon grated lemon peel
> 1 teaspoon cinnamon

- Preheat oven to 400°.
- Beat cream cheese, sugar, egg yolk and vanilla in small mixing bowl at medium speed with electric mixer until well blended.
- Rinse and drain blueberries. Stir together muffin mix, water, egg and peel in large bowl (mixture will be lumpy). Fold in blueberries. Pour into well greased medium-sized muffin pan.
- Spoon cream cheese mixture over batter; sprinkle with combined topping mix and cinnamon.
- Bake 18 to 22 minutes or until lightly browned. Cool 5 minutes. Loosen muffins from rim of pan; cool before removing from pan.   *1 dozen*

Prep time: 20 minutes
Cooking time: 22 minutes

Top: Homestyle Blueberry Muffins;
bottom: Caramel Pecan Sticky Buns (page 60)

CARAMEL PECAN STICKY BUNS

"PHILLY" Cream Cheese adds its special flavor to the dough.

1 8-oz. pkg. PHILADELPHIA BRAND Cream
    Cheese, cubed
¾ cup cold water
1 16-oz. pkg. hot roll mix
1 egg
⅓ cup granulated sugar
1 teaspoon cinnamon
1 cup pecan halves
¾ cup packed brown sugar
½ cup light corn syrup
¼ cup PARKAY Margarine, melted

- Preheat oven to 350°.
- Stir together 6 ounces cream cheese and water in small saucepan. Cook over low heat until mixture reaches 115° to 120°, stirring occasionally.
- Stir together hot roll mix and yeast packet in large bowl. Add cream cheese mixture and egg, mixing until dough pulls away from sides of bowl.
- Knead dough on lightly floured surface 5 minutes or until smooth and elastic. Cover; let rise in warm place 20 minutes.
- Beat remaining cream cheese, granulated sugar and cinnamon in small mixing bowl at medium speed with electric mixer until well blended.
- Roll out dough to 18×12-inch rectangle; spread cream cheese mixture over dough to within 1 inch from outer edges of dough.
- Roll up from long end; sealing edges. Cut into twenty-four ¾ inch slices.
- Stir together remaining ingredients in small bowl. Spoon 2 teaspoonfuls mixture into bottoms of greased medium-sized muffin pans.
- Place dough, cut side up, in cups. Cover; let rise in warm place 30 minutes.
- Bake 20 to 25 minutes or until golden brown. Invert onto serving platter immediately.

2 dozen

Prep time: 30 minutes plus rising
Cooking time: 25 minutes

PIÑA COLADA COFFEECAKE

¼ cup chopped almonds
¼ cup packed brown sugar
¼ cup BAKER'S ANGEL FLAKE Coconut
2 tablespoons flour
1 teaspoon cinnamon
1 10-oz. container frozen piña colada fruit
    mixer concentrate, thawed
1 8-oz. pkg. PHILADELPHIA BRAND Cream
    Cheese, softened
2 tablespoons lime juice
3 eggs
1 18.25-oz. pkg. white cake mix
    Lime Glaze

- Preheat oven 350°.
- Stir together almonds, brown sugar, coconut,
  flour and cinnamon in small bowl.
- Reserve 3 tablespoons piña colada concentrate
  for use in Lime Glaze. Beat cream cheese,
  remaining concentrate and 2 tablespoons lime
  juice in large mixing bowl at medium speed with
  electric mixer until well blended.
- Add eggs, one at a time, mixing well after each
  addition. Add cake mix; beat until well blended.
- Pour half of batter into greased and floured
  10-inch fluted tube pan. Sprinkle almond
  mixture over batter; top with remaining batter.
- Bake 55 to 60 minutes or until wooden pick
  inserted in center comes out clean. Cool. Drizzle
  with Lime Glaze.   *10 to 12 servings*

LIME GLAZE

3 tablespoons reserved piña colada
    concentrate
2 teaspoons lime juice
1½ cups sifted powdered sugar

- Stir together reserved concentrate and
  2 teaspoons lime juice in small bowl until
  smooth; gradually stir in powdered sugar.

Prep time: 25 minutes
Cooking time: 1 hour

Ovens are ideal for rising yeast breads. A gas oven warmed by the pilot or an electric oven turned to the lowest setting 1 minute, then turned off will provide enough warmth for rising.

ORANGE RUM BABA

1 8-oz. pkg. PHILADELPHIA BRAND Cream Cheese, cubed
1 cup orange juice
2 tablespoons PARKAY Margarine
2 tablespoons sugar
1 teaspoon grated orange peel
1 tablespoon rum
1 16-oz. pkg. hot roll mix
1 egg
2 cups cold water
1 cup sugar
3 tablespoons rum
2 tablespoons vanilla
    Orange Glaze

- Preheat oven to 350°.
- Stir together cream cheese, juice, margarine, 2 tablespoons sugar and peel in small saucepan. Cook over low heat until mixture reaches 115° to 120°, stirring occasionally. Stir in 1 tablespoon rum.
- Stir together hot roll mix and yeast packet in large bowl. Add cream cheese mixture and egg, mixing until dough pulls away from the sides of bowl.
- Knead dough on lightly floured surface 5 minutes or until smooth and elastic. Cover; let rise in warm place 20 minutes.
- Place dough in greased 6½-cup ring mold. Cover; let rise in warm place until double in volume, about 35 minutes.
- Bake 30 to 35 minutes or until golden brown. Cool slightly.
- Stir together water and 1 cup sugar in small saucepan over low heat until sugar is dissolved. Stir in 3 tablespoons rum and vanilla. Reserve ¾ cup syrup for use in Orange Glaze.
- Prick cake several times with fork. Pour 1 cup remaining syrup over cake; let stand 15 minutes. Invert onto rimmed plate; prick cake several times with fork. Pour remaining syrup over cake. Drizzle with Orange Glaze. Serve with whipped cream and seasonal fruit, if desired.

10 to 12 servings

(continued on next page)

ORANGE GLAZE

¾ cup reserved syrup
1 tablespoon cornstarch
1 teaspoon orange zest

- Gradually add reserved syrup to cornstarch in small saucepan.
- Bring to boil over medium heat, stirring constantly. Boil 1 minute. Stir in zest.

Prep time: 45 minutes plus rising
Cooking time: 35 minutes

PEAR CREAM BREAKFAST CAKE

Incredibly delicious ... perfect for brunch or as a delicious dessert.

1 29-oz. can pear halves in heavy syrup, undrained
1 8-oz. pkg. PHILADELPHIA BRAND Cream Cheese, softened
¼ cup KRAFT Apricot Preserves
2 tablespoons PARKAY Margarine
1 9-oz. pkg. yellow cake mix
2 tablespoons oil
1 egg
1 teaspoon ground ginger

- Preheat oven to 350°.
- Drain pears, reserving ½ cup syrup. Slice pears; place on bottom of 8-inch square baking pan.
- Beat cream cheese, preserves and margarine in small mixing bowl at medium speed with electric mixer until well blended; pour over pears.
- Beat cake mix, reserved syrup, oil, egg and ginger in large mixing bowl at low speed with electric mixer until well blended; pour over cream cheese mixture.
- Bake 35 to 40 minutes or until golden brown. Serve warm with half and half.

8 to 10 servings

Prep time: 15 minutes
Cooking time: 40 minutes

Pear Cream Breakfast Cake

DESSERTS

It's hard to think of luscious, tempting desserts without thinking of PHILADELPHIA BRAND Cream Cheese. Although "PHILLY" Cream Cheese is famous for cheesecakes, it is also the secret ingredient in a wide range of spoonable desserts, creamy sauces and toppings, luscious fillings and chewy bars. Enjoy our collection of recipes on the following pages!

BANANA BERRY BROWNIE PIZZA

A fresh fruit pizza with a brownie crust is a guaranteed success at any party.

⅓ cup cold water
1 15-oz. pkg. brownie mix
¼ cup oil
1 egg
1 8-oz. pkg. PHILADELPHIA BRAND Cream Cheese, softened
¼ cup sugar
1 egg
1 teaspoon vanilla
  Strawberry slices
  Banana slices
2 1-oz. squares BAKER'S Semi-Sweet Chocolate, melted

- Preheat oven to 350°.
- Bring water to boil.
- Mix together brownie mix, water, oil and egg in large bowl until well blended.
- Pour into greased and floured 12-inch pizza pan.
- Bake 25 minutes.
- Beat cream cheese, sugar, egg and vanilla in small mixing bowl at medium speed with electric mixer until well blended. Pour over crust.
- Bake 15 minutes. Cool. Top with fruit; drizzle with chocolate. Garnish with mint leaves, if desired.   *10 to 12 servings*

Prep time: 35 minutes
Cooking time: 40 minutes

Microwave Tip: To melt chocolate, place unwrapped chocolate squares in small bowl. Microwave on HIGH 1 to 2 minutes or until almost melted. Stir until smooth.

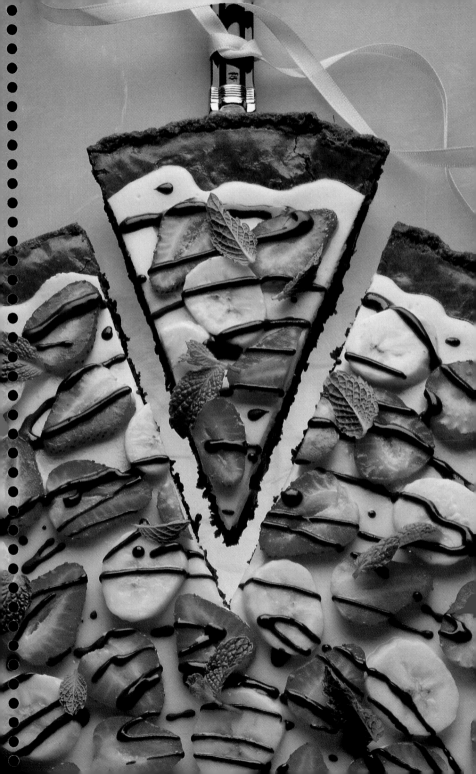

CITRUS FRUIT CHEESECAKE

Assorted fresh fruit makes a festive topping for this traditional baked cheesecake with a hint of orange.

1 cup graham cracker crumbs
⅓ cup packed brown sugar
¼ cup PARKAY Margarine, melted
4 8-oz. pkgs. PHILADELPHIA BRAND
    Cream Cheese, softened
1 cup sugar
4 eggs
2 tablespoons shredded orange peel
    Assorted fresh fruit

- Preheat oven to 325°.
- Stir together crumbs, sugar and margarine in small bowl; press onto bottom of 9-inch springform pan. Bake 10 minutes.
- Beat cream cheese and sugar in large mixing bowl at medium speed with electric mixer until well blended.
- Add eggs, one at a time, mixing well after each addition. Blend in peel; pour over crust.
- Bake 50 minutes.
- Loosen cake from rim of pan; cool before removing rim of pan. Chill.
- Top with fruit. Garnish with lime peel, if desired.

10 to 12 servings

Prep time: 20 minutes plus chilling
Cooking time: 50 minutes

Star fruit or carambola is a natural beauty. Its flavors range from slightly tart to sweet. Select firm, shiny fruit and allow to ripen at room temperature. Browning along the edges is a sign of ripening. Slice cross-wise to form stars; do not peel.

BUTTERSCOTCH PEANUT BARS

These bars are sure to be a kid's favorite that adults will love too!

> 1 8-oz. pkg. PHILADELPHIA BRAND Cream Cheese, softened
> ½ cup packed brown sugar
> ½ cup granulated sugar
> ¼ cup PARKAY Margarine
> ½ cup milk
> 1 egg
> 2 teaspoons vanilla
> 2¼ cups flour
> 1 teaspoon CALUMET Baking Powder
> ¼ teaspoon salt
> 1 cup chopped salted peanuts
> 1 cup butterscotch artificial flavored morsels
> Butterscotch Frosting
> ½ cup chopped salted peanuts

- Preheat oven to 350°.
- Beat cream cheese, sugars and ¼ cup margarine in large mixing bowl at medium speed with electric mixer until well blended. Blend in ½ cup milk, egg and vanilla.
- Add combined dry ingredients; mix well. Stir in 1 cup peanuts and 1 cup butterscotch morsels. Spread into greased 15×10×1-inch jelly roll pan.
- Bake 20 to 25 minutes or until wooden pick inserted in center comes out clean. Spread with Butterscotch Frosting. Sprinkle with ½ cup peanuts. Cut into bars.

Approximately 3 dozen

BUTTERSCOTCH FROSTING

> 1 cup butterscotch artificial flavored morsels
> ½ cup creamy peanut butter
> 2 tablespoons PARKAY Margarine
> 1 tablespoon milk

- Stir together all ingredients in small saucepan over low heat until smooth.

Prep time: 20 minutes
Cooking time: 25 minutes

SUNSHINE FRUIT TARTS

1 15-oz. pkg. PILLSBURY All Ready Pie
    Crusts
⅓ cup KRAFT Pineapple Preserves
⅓ cup KRAFT Strawberry Preserves
1 8-oz. container PHILADELPHIA BRAND
    Soft Cream Cheese with Pineapple
1 8-oz. container PHILADELPHIA BRAND
    Soft Cream Cheese with Strawberries

- Preheat oven to 450°.
- Roll each pie crust on lightly floured surface to
  15-inch circle; cut each circle into eighteen
  circles with 3-inch cookie cutter. Place in
  miniature muffin pans or individual miniature
  tart pans; trim excess dough. Prick bottom and
  sides with fork.
- Bake 8 to 10 minutes or until lightly browned.
  Cool. Remove from pans.
- Spoon scant teaspoonful of preserves into each
  pastry shell; top with cream cheese. Garnish
  with sliced fruit, orange peel and mint leaves, if
  desired.   *3 dozen*

Prep time: 35 minutes
Cooking time: 10 minutes

Tip: Pipe cream cheese into pastry shells using
pastry tube with star tip.

LEMON CHEESECAKE SQUARES

1¼ cups (18 to 19) shortbread cookie crumbs
 ⅓ cup ground almonds
 3 tablespoons PARKAY Margarine, melted
 2 tablespoons sugar
 1 6-oz. container frozen lemonade
    concentrate, thawed
 3 8-oz. pkgs. PHILADELPHIA BRAND
    Cream Cheese, softened
 1 cup sour cream
 1 3½-oz. pkg. JELL-O Brand Lemon Flavor
    Instant Pudding and Pie Filling
 2 cups COOL WHIP Non-Dairy Whipped
    Topping, thawed

- Preheat oven to 350°.
- Stir together crumbs, almonds, margarine and sugar in small bowl; press onto bottom of 13×9-inch baking pan. Bake 10 minutes. Cool.
- Gradually add lemonade concentrate to cream cheese in large mixing bowl, mixing at low speed with electric mixer until well blended. Add sour cream and pudding mix; beat 1 minute.
- Fold in whipped topping; pour over crust.
- Freeze until firm. Cut into squares. Garnish with fresh berries and mint, if desired.

18 servings

Prep time: 15 minutes plus freezing

LEMON NUT BARS

1⅓ cups flour
½ cup packed brown sugar
¼ cup granulated sugar
¾ cup PARKAY Margarine
1 cup old fashioned or quick oats, uncooked
½ cup chopped nuts
1 8-oz. pkg. PHILADELPHIA BRAND Cream Cheese, softened
1 egg
3 tablespoons lemon juice
1 tablespoon grated lemon peel

- Preheat oven to 350°.
- Stir together flour and sugars in medium bowl. Cut in margarine until mixture resembles coarse crumbs. Stir in oats and nuts.
- Reserve 1 cup crumb mixture; press remaining crumb mixture onto bottom of greased 13×9-inch baking pan. Bake 15 minutes.
- Beat cream cheese, egg, juice and peel in small mixing bowl at medium speed with electric mixer until well blended. Pour over crust; sprinkle with reserved crumb mixture.
- Bake 25 minutes. Cool; cut into bars.

Approximately 3 dozen

Prep time: 30 minutes
Cooking time: 25 minutes

Lemon Nut Bars

COFFEE TOFFEE PIE

Crushed toffee bars and coffee liqueur are the flavor highlights of this "make-in-minutes" cheesecake pie.

2 cups chocolate wafer crumbs
¼ cup sugar
6 tablespoons PARKAY Margarine, melted
1 8-oz. pkg. PHILADELPHIA BRAND Cream Cheese, softened
3 to 4 tablespoons coffee flavored liqueur
1 8-oz. container COOL WHIP Non-Dairy Whipped Topping, thawed
4 1.4-oz. (1 cup) milk chocolate covered toffee bars, chopped

- Preheat oven to 350°.
- Stir together crumbs, sugar and margarine in medium bowl; press onto bottom and up sides of 9-inch pie plate. Bake 10 minutes.
- Beat cream cheese and liqueur in large mixing bowl at medium speed with electric mixer until well blended. Fold in whipped topping and ¾ cup candy; pour into crust.
- Sprinkle with remaining candy. Chill until firm.

8 to 10 servings

Prep time: 10 minutes plus chilling

S'MORE CHEESECAKE

This special cheesecake is an update of the timeless camp favorite — everyone will want "s'more"!

1¼ cups graham cracker crumbs
⅓ cup PARKAY Margarine, melted
¼ cup sugar
1 12-oz. container PHILADELPHIA BRAND Soft Cream Cheese
5 1.45-oz. milk chocolate candy bars, melted
1 1.45-oz. milk chocolate candy bar, finely chopped
1 cup KRAFT Miniature Marshmallows
1½ cups COOL WHIP Non-Dairy Whipped Topping, thawed

Coffee Toffee Pie

- Stir together crumbs, margarine and sugar in small bowl; press onto bottom and 1 inch up sides of 9-inch springform pan. Chill.
- Stir together cream cheese and melted chocolate in small bowl until well blended; pour into crust. Sprinkle with chopped chocolate.
- Fold marshmallows into whipped topping; spread over cheesecake. Chill.   *10 to 12 servings*

Prep time: 15 minutes plus chilling

Tip: Chill candy bar before chopping.

PEANUTTY HOT FUDGE CHEESECAKE

This cheesecake is destined to become a family favorite.

1½ cups graham cracker crumbs
⅓ cup PARKAY Margarine, melted
¼ cup granulated sugar
1 8-oz. pkg. PHILADELPHIA BRAND Cream Cheese, softened
1 cup powdered sugar
⅓ cup peanut butter
3 cups COOL WHIP Non-Dairy Whipped Topping, thawed
¼ cup chopped peanuts
¼ cup KRAFT Hot Fudge Topping, heated

- Preheat oven to 350°.
- Stir together crumbs, margarine and granulated sugar in small bowl; press onto bottom and ½ inch up sides of 9-inch springform pan. Bake 10 minutes. Cool.
- Beat cream cheese, powdered sugar and peanut butter in large mixing bowl at medium speed with electric mixer until well blended.
- Fold in whipped topping; pour into crust. Sprinkle with peanuts. Chill until firm.
- Drizzle topping over cheesecake just before serving.   *10 to 12 servings*

Prep time: 15 minutes plus chilling

Peanutty Hot Fudge Cheesecake

WHITE MOUSSE WITH RASPBERRY SAUCE

This dessert can be made especially elegant when served as an individual molded dessert.

½ cup milk
1 cup (8 ozs.) ready to spread vanilla frosting
1 envelope unflavored gelatin
¼ cup milk
1 12-oz. container PHILADELPHIA BRAND
    Soft Cream Cheese
2 teaspoons vanilla
2 egg whites, room temperature
¼ teaspoon salt
½ cup whipping cream
    Raspberry Sauce

- Mix together ½ cup milk and frosting in medium saucepan, stirring constantly. Remove from heat.
- Soften gelatin in ¼ cup milk in small saucepan; stir over low heat until dissolved. Add to frosting mixture; cool.
- Beat cream cheese and vanilla in large mixing bowl at medium speed with electric mixer until well blended. Blend in frosting mixture.
- Beat egg whites and salt in small mixing bowl at high speed with electric mixer until stiff peaks form. In separate bowl, beat whipping cream with electric mixer at high speed until soft peaks form.
- Fold egg whites and whipped cream into cream cheese mixture.
- Pour into lightly oiled 1½ to 2-quart mold; chill until firm. Unmold; serve with Raspberry Sauce.

14 to 16 servings

RASPBERRY SAUCE

1 10-oz. pkg. BIRDS EYE Quick Thaw Red
    Raspberries in a Lite Syrup, thawed
½ cup KRAFT Red Currant Jelly
4 teaspoons cornstarch

- Place raspberries and jelly in food processor or blender container; process until well blended. Strain.
- Stir together cornstarch and raspberry mixture in small saucepan until smooth.
- Bring to boil over medium heat, stirring constantly. Cook until thickened, stirring constantly. Cool.

Prep time: 25 minutes plus chilling
Cooking time: 10 minutes

Microwave Tip: To dissolve gelatin, soften gelatin in milk. Microwave on HIGH 30 to 45 seconds or until dissolved, stirring every 15 seconds.

MADISON AVENUE MOCHA BROWNIES

Very sophisticated... easy brownies made from a mix, but marbled with a mocha blend of coffee and sweetened cream cheese.

    1 20 to 23-oz. pkg. brownie mix
    1 8-oz. pkg. PHILADELPHIA BRAND Cream
        Cheese, softened
    ⅓ cup sugar
    1 egg
    1½ teaspoons MAXWELL HOUSE Instant
        Coffee
    1 teaspoon vanilla

- Preheat oven to 350°.
- Prepare brownie mix according to package directions. Pour into greased 13×9-inch baking pan.
- Beat cream cheese, sugar and egg in small mixing bowl at medium speed with electric mixer until well blended.
- Dissolve coffee in vanilla; add to cream cheese mixture, mixing until well blended.
- Spoon cream cheese mixture over brownie batter; cut through batter with knife several times for marble effect.
- Bake 35 to 40 minutes or until cream cheese mixture is set.   *4 dozen*

Prep time: 20 minutes
Cooking time: 40 minutes

MARBLE CHEESECAKE SQUARES

(pictured on back cover)

1 cup flour
1 cup chopped hazelnuts
½ cup PARKAY Margarine
⅓ cup packed brown sugar
¼ teaspoon almond extract
3 8-oz. pkgs. PHILADELPHIA BRAND
     Cream Cheese, softened
¾ cup granulated sugar
1 teaspoon vanilla
1 tablespoon orange flavored liqueur
3 eggs
1 1-oz. square BAKER'S Unsweetened
     Chocolate, melted

To soften cream cheese, microwave in bowl on MEDIUM (50%) 30 seconds for each 8 ounce package.

- Preheat oven to 325°.
- Beat flour, hazelnuts, margarine, brown sugar and extract in small mixing bowl at medium speed with electric mixer until well blended. Press onto bottom of 9-inch square baking pan. Bake 8 to 10 minutes or until lightly browned.
- Beat cream cheese, granulated sugar, vanilla and liqueur in large mixing bowl at medium speed with electric mixer until well blended.
- Add eggs, one at a time, mixing well after each addition.
- Blend chocolate into 1 cup batter; pour remaining batter over crust. Place chocolate batter in pastry tube. Pipe six strips on top of batter; cut through batter with knife several times for marble effect.
- Bake 30 to 35 minutes or until set. Chill.

15 servings

Prep time: 15 minutes plus chilling
Cooking time: 35 minutes

BANANA CHOCOLATE MINI CHEESECAKES

12 creme-filled chocolate cookies
1 8-oz. pkg. PHILADELPHIA BRAND Cream Cheese, softened
⅓ cup sugar
1 teaspoon lemon juice
2 eggs
½ cup mashed ripe banana
2 ozs. BAKER'S German Sweet Chocolate, broken into pieces
1½ tablespoons cold water
1½ tablespoons PARKAY Margarine
Banana slices

- Preheat oven to 350°.
- Place one cookie onto bottom of each of twelve paper-lined muffin cups.
- Beat cream cheese, sugar and juice in large mixing bowl at medium speed with electric mixer until well blended.
- Add eggs, one at a time, mixing after each addition. Blend in mashed banana; pour over cookies, filling each cup ¾ full.
- Bake 15 to 20 minutes or until set.
- Melt chocolate with water in small saucepan over low heat, stirring constantly. Remove from heat; stir in margarine until melted. Cool.
- Top cheesecakes with banana slices just before serving; drizzle with chocolate mixture.

12 servings

Prep time: 15 minutes
Cooking time: 20 minutes

CHOCOLATE TRUFFLE CHEESECAKE

(pictured on front cover)

Try this totally chocolate cheesecake...from the crisp wafer crust to the smooth creamy center to the rich chocolate topping.

1 cup chocolate wafer crumbs
3 tablespoons PARKAY Margarine, melted
2 8-oz. pkgs. PHILADELPHIA BRAND
    Cream Cheese, softened
⅔ cup sugar
2 eggs
1 cup BAKER'S Real Semi-Sweet Chocolate
    Chips, melted
½ teaspoon vanilla
    Creamy Raspberry Sauce

* Preheat oven to 350°.
* Stir together crumbs and margarine in small bowl; press onto bottom of 9-inch springform pan. Bake 10 minutes.
* Beat cream cheese and sugar in large mixing bowl at medium speed with electric mixer until well blended.
* Add eggs, one at a time, mixing well after each addition.
* Blend in chocolate chips and vanilla; pour over crust.
* Bake 45 minutes. Loosen cake from rim of pan; cool before removing rim of pan. Chill.
* Spoon Creamy Raspberry Sauce onto each serving plate. Place slice of cheesecake over sauce. Garnish as desired.   *10 to 12 servings*

CREAMY RASPBERRY SAUCE

1 10-oz. pkg. BIRDS EYE Quick Thaw Red
    Raspberries in a Lite Syrup, thawed
3 tablespoons whipping cream

* Place raspberries in food processor or blender container; process until smooth. Strain. Stir in cream.

Prep time: 30 minutes plus chilling
Cooking time: 45 minutes

A dusting of powdered sugar or cocoa is an attractive topping for bar cookies or cheesecakes. Place a paper doily or paper strips over the dessert. Sift powdered sugar onto the dessert. Carefully remove the doily or paper strips.

ALMOND CHEESECAKE WITH RASPBERRIES

This quick and easy dessert can be prepared in advance for elegant entertaining.

1¼ cups graham cracker crumbs
  ¼ cup PARKAY Margarine, melted
  ¼ cup sugar
  2 8-oz. pkgs. PHILADELPHIA BRAND
      Cream Cheese, softened
  1 16-oz. can ready to spread vanilla frosting
  1 tablespoon lemon juice
  1 tablespoon grated lemon peel
  3 cups COOL WHIP Non-Dairy Whipped
      Topping, thawed
    Raspberries
    Sliced almonds

- Stir together crumbs, margarine and sugar in small bowl; press onto bottom and ½ inch up sides of 9-inch springform pan or pie plate. Chill.
- Beat cream cheese, frosting, juice and peel in large mixing bowl at medium speed with electric mixer until well blended.
- Fold in whipped topping; pour into crust. Chill until firm.
- Arrange raspberries and almonds on top of cheesecake. Garnish with fresh mint, if desired.

10 to 12 servings

Prep time: 30 minutes plus chilling

WALNUT SHORTBREAD BARS

  1 8-oz. pkg. PHILADELPHIA BRAND Cream
      Cheese, softened
  1 cup PARKAY Margarine
  ¾ cup granulated sugar
  ¾ cup packed brown sugar
  1 egg
  1 teaspoon vanilla
2½ cups flour
  1 teaspoon CALUMET Baking Powder
  ½ teaspoon salt
  ¾ cup chopped walnuts

Almond Cheesecake with Raspberries

- Preheat oven to 350°.
- Beat cream cheese, margarine and sugars in large mixing bowl at medium speed with electric mixer until well blended. Blend in egg and vanilla.
- Add combined dry ingredients; mix well. Stir in walnuts. Spread into greased 15×10×1-inch jelly roll pan.
- Bake 20 to 25 minutes or until lightly browned. Cool. Sprinkle with powdered sugar, if desired. Cut into bars.   *Approximately 5 dozen*

Prep time: 15 minutes
Cooking time: 25 minutes

SPRING FLING FRUIT TART

    1 cup flour
   ¼ cup packed brown sugar
   ½ cup PARKAY Margarine
    1 8-oz. pkg. PHILADELPHIA BRAND Cream Cheese, softened
   ¼ cup granulated sugar
    1 tablespoon grated orange peel
   ¾ cup whipping cream, whipped
     Peeled Kiwi slices
     Strawberry halves

- Preheat oven to 350°.
- Stir together flour and brown sugar in medium bowl. Cut in margarine until mixture resembles coarse crumbs; knead mixture until well blended. Press onto bottom and ½ inch up sides of 10-inch tart pan with removable bottom.
- Bake 15 minutes or until golden brown. Cool.
- Beat cream cheese, granulated sugar and peel in large mixing bowl at medium speed with electric mixer until well blended. Fold in whipped cream; pour into crust. Chill until firm.
- Arrange fruit on top of tart just before serving. Carefully remove rim of pan.
                                    10 to 12 servings

Prep time: 30 minutes plus chilling

Tip: When preparing crust, wet fingertips in cold water before pressing crumb mixture into pan.

Spring Fling Fruit Tart

AMARETTO BREEZE

Easy elegance... for a refreshing change, serve the sauce with melon balls, raspberries, sliced peaches or a combination of these fruits.

> 1 8-oz. pkg. PHILADELPHIA BRAND Cream
>   Cheese, softened
> ½ cup sour cream
> ½ cup sugar
> 3 tablespoons almond flavored liqueur
> 2 tablespoons whipping cream
> 1 pt. blackberries or blueberries
> 1 pt. strawberries

- Beat cream cheese and sour cream in small mixing bowl at medium speed with electric mixer until well blended. Blend in sugar, liqueur and cream. Chill.
- Place berries in individual serving dishes; top with cream cheese sauce.　　*4 to 6 servings*

Prep time: 10 minutes plus chilling

STRAWBERRY COOL

This springtime dessert is easy to prepare and tastes so good. The family will love it.

> 1 10-oz. pkg. BIRDS EYE Quick Thaw
>   Strawberries in Syrup, partially thawed
> ¼ cup whipping cream
> 1 8-oz. container PHILADELPHIA BRAND
>   Soft Cream Cheese with Strawberries
> 1 cup (7 to 8) coarsley crumbled pecan
>   shortbread cookies

- Place strawberries and whipping cream in food processor or blender container; process until well blended.
- Add cream cheese; process until just blended.
- Alternately layer cookie crumbs and strawberry mixture in individual parfait or sherbet glasses. Chill. Garnish with additional whipped cream, if desired.　　*4 servings*

Prep time: 10 minutes plus chilling

Amaretto Breeze

CHEESECAKE MACAROON BARS

These bars are a great treat for afternoon tea, brunch or a casual party.

1 cup flour
1 cup ground almonds
½ cup PARKAY Margarine
⅓ cup packed brown sugar
¼ teaspoon salt
¼ teaspoon almond extract
2 8-oz. pkgs. PHILADELPHIA BRAND
    Cream Cheese, softened
¾ cup granulated sugar
1 tablespoon lemon juice
3 eggs
1 cup BAKER'S ANGEL FLAKE Coconut,
    toasted
1½ cups sour cream
3 tablespoons granulated sugar
2 teaspoons vanilla
½ cup BAKER'S ANGEL FLAKE Coconut,
    toasted

- Preheat oven to 350°.
- Beat flour, almonds, margarine, brown sugar, salt and extract in small mixing bowl at medium speed with electric mixer until well blended. Press onto bottom of 13×9-inch baking pan.
- Bake 8 to 10 minutes or until lightly browned.
- Beat cream cheese, ¾ cup granulated sugar and lemon juice in large mixing bowl at medium speed with electric mixer until well blended.
- Add eggs, one at a time, mixing well after each addition. Stir in 1 cup coconut; pour over crust.
- Bake 25 minutes. Cool 5 minutes.
- Stir together sour cream, 3 tablespoons granulated sugar and vanilla in small bowl until smooth; carefully spread over coconut mixture.
- Bake 5 to 7 minutes or until set. Sprinkle with ½ cup coconut; cool. Cut into bars.

Approximately 3 dozen

Prep time: 30 minutes plus cooling
Cooking time: 32 minutes

Cheesecake Macaroon Bars

CLASSIC CHEESECAKE

⅓ cup PARKAY Margarine
⅓ cup sugar
1 egg
1¼ cups flour
2 8-oz. pkgs. PHILADELPHIA BRAND
   Cream Cheese, softened
½ cup sugar
1 tablespoon lemon juice
1 teaspoon grated lemon peel
½ teaspoon vanilla
3 eggs
1 cup sour cream
1 tablespoon sugar
1 teaspoon vanilla

- Preheat oven to 450°.
- Beat margarine and ⅓ cup sugar until light and fluffy; blend in one egg. Add flour; mix well.
- Spread dough onto bottom and 1½ inches up sides of 9-inch springform pan. Bake 5 minutes.
- Beat cream cheese, ½ cup sugar, juice, peel and ½ teaspoon vanilla in large mixing bowl at medium speed with electric mixer until well blended.
- Add three eggs, one at a time, mixing well after each addition; pour into crust.
- Bake 50 minutes.
- Stir together sour cream, 1 tablespoon sugar and 1 teaspoon vanilla in small bowl. Spread evenly over cake; continue baking 10 minutes. Loosen cake from rim of pan; cool before removing rim of pan. Chill.
- Serve with BIRDS EYE Frozen Quick Thaw Strawberries in Syrup, thawed, if desired.

10 to 12 servings

Prep time: 30 minutes plus chilling
Cooking time: 1 hour

Truly a "PHILLY classic", this often requested cheesecake recipe has been a family favorite for years. No "PHILLY" Cream Cheese recipe collection would be complete without this simple and elegant grand finale.

You can determine that a cheesecake is done baking when the top has lost its sheen.

To lessen the effect of cracking, allow cheesecake to cool 5 minutes. Insert thin metal spatula between cake or crust and rim of pan; run spatula around inside edge to loosen cake.

INDEX